Musings of a Minnesota Farm Boy

Written by David Alton Johnson

— INTRODUCTION —

Musings of a Minnesota Farm Boy was birthed from the memories of myself, the author. They are memories of life growing up on a turkey farm in Minnesota during the 50s and 60s. It was a great time to be a kid in America. These were the baby boom years, a time when America was living the American dream and families were taking advantage of a good economy after the war years. Of course there were problems in America too. Race relations, particularly in the south under Jim Crow Laws, were appalling. The Korean War in the early 50s was also painful, especially for those whose loved ones fought and died. Still, my childhood was definitely a "Leave it to Beaver" life, and I benefitted from it immensely. Life was simple growing up on the farm, and I loved it.

Writing these memories or musings, I hope to leave a legacy for my children and grandchildren, a legacy of a simple, happy life that is probably much rarer today than when I grew up as a Minnesota farm boy.

— Chapter One —
The Turkey Farm

My dad owned a turkey farm where he raised thousands of turkeys each year. Dad had a 160-acre parcel of land, where he also raised alfalfa and wheat and oats.

Raising turkeys was an awesome deal. Dad had a brooder barn where the baby chicks started out. He bought the young chicks from the turkey nursery, several thousand at a time. The brooder barn had wire mesh flooring, which allowed the waste (turkey poop) to drop through onto the dirt floor beneath.

The baby chicks needed warmth to survive, and this was accomplished with large propane heaters wired in place over the baby chicks to keep them warm and cozy.

They also needed water and food to grow. The water containers were one-gallon jugs filled with water and tipped upside down over a glass plate. This allowed for water to be served continually. Their feed was crushed grain served in small trays.

Young turkey chicks were the cutest things. Of course, with so many chicks there were bound to be some that died for whatever reason. One of my jobs was to remove the dead chicks and throw them into garbage bags made of leftover grain bags.

The baby chicks grew fast. When the turkeys were several weeks old, Dad would allow them to go onto a patio outside that was connected to the brooder house. When they were large enough, they were moved to the alfalfa fields. Turkeys love to eat fresh alfalfa!

In the alfalfa fields were sheds where the turkeys could find cover from the rain and rest in the night. My dad and my older brother Ron, with help from neighbors, built these outdoor turkey sheds. They used logs as skids on which the framing was built. Finally, they nailed galvanized tin roofing to the framing to make a rainproof roof shelter for the turkeys. Several of these sheds sat side by side and could be moved to new ground by tractors when the turkeys ate all the alfalfa in one location.

I had a small part in making these sheds. I remember using a log peeler which scraped the bark from the skid logs. That's the way it was on the farm growing up... everybody, even young kids, participated in the work.

It was a great way to live.

Raising turkeys was a family affair. Even though I was a youngster, I was expected to do my part. They were called "chores," and everyone in the family had a part. At age eight, I was responsible to help feed the turkeys. I filled grain feeders and water feeders. Filling those water feeders led to one of the more traumatic incidents in my life. Here is how it happened.

My mother was driving the water truck. It was an old 1937 Ford truck with a 500-gallon water tank attached behind the cab. I was lying on the bed of the truck next to the water tank. Why I was there I don't remember, but I was watching my mom approach the pole barn. As she drove up the slight incline, she killed the engine. The truck began to roll backwards and when mom put on the brakes, it lurched to a stop, but the water tank rolled out of its cradle right on top of me! The only thing that saved me from being crushed by the 500-gallon tank of water was a fencing maul wedged on top of a bucket that served as a lever against the bucket. The bucket was crushed by the weight of the water tank. I lay face up, the water tank pinning me against the bed of the truck. My mother jumped up onto the truck and pushed against the water tank. "Help me! I don't want to die!" I begged. I really thought it was over for me. Whenever mom let up from pushing on the tank, I cried in terror, "I don't want to die!"

My older sister Irene jumped on a bike, rode to the neighbors, and told them I was under the water tank. The neighbors came running and pulled me out from under the water tank. Meanwhile, my dad was walking in from the field where he had been plowing. He was walking at a leisurely pace, because when my cousin Arlan told him the tank fell over, he failed to mention that the tank rolled on top of me!

My parents loaded me in the car and took me to the doctor's office to have me examined. My only injuries were a scraped tummy and pinched toes!

This was my first brush with death. Several years later I would survive a river excursion where I could easily have drowned.

— Chapter two —
SCHOOL

When I was five years old, I started first grade. There was no kindergarten. My older brothers and sisters and I attended a two-room country schoolhouse. One room was for storage and for inside recess when it was too wet or too cold to play outside. The other room was the classroom where we had one teacher who taught grades 1-8. There was a huge gas or oil furnace in the back of the schoolhouse and a small backroom where the water fountain was.

Our teacher was Mrs. Henstorf, a middle-aged woman. She was a no nonsense, firm discipline 1950's type of teacher. I was born in December of 1952, so this was in the fall of 1958. I still have my picture from first grade, flannel shirt and all!

Mrs. Henstorf started each day reading from a book. Old Yeller is the book I remember most. For those who haven't read it or seen the movie, Old Yeller is about a yellow colored stray dog that a country family adopts as their own. Old Yeller, as he was called, contracts rabies from a wolf he was fighting to defend the family, and the young man in the story has to shoot Old Yeller because of the rabies. It is a sad ending to a great story.

When I started first grade, I had only two classmates, Michael Meyers and Brenda Olson. Michael ended up flunking first grade. Through the fifth grade, when my family moved away, Brenda was my only classmate. She was also a distant cousin. I should mention that only about 20 students attended the one-room country school, and half of them were in some way related to me, mostly cousins of one sort or another.

After reading, Mrs. Henstorf taught one grade and subject at a time, by having each grade come forward to the front table. For several minutes, she would lead the students, teaching us the lesson for the day and then dismissing us and moving on to the next group. She started with first grade and moved on up to the eighth grade. While students waited to be called forward, they read silently or did other classwork. Mrs. Henstorf kept a well-disciplined environment in the classroom. I don't ever remember a time when students were noisy or disruptive.

If you were thirsty and needed a drink of water, you

could leave the main classroom and go to the back room where a gravity fed drinking water fountain was available. This water was hauled into the backroom by older students during chore time at the beginning of each day. There was no indoor plumbing or indoor toilets, only a girls' outdoor toilet and a boys' privy as well. Drinking water came from an old outdoor pump from a well beneath the ground. Water was hauled inside with 5-gallon buckets and poured into a container inside the back room of the school house. This was all gravity fed to a drinking fountain and cold water sink. Quite primitive, wasn't it? Welcome to the 1950s and country living.

My siblings and I walked to and from school each day, about a one-mile walk each way. Even in the winter time, we walked! It wasn't until I was in the 3rd or 4th grade that the school purchased a bus. The school bus was a 40s model wood panel van. From then on we no longer had to walk.

School was usually held regardless of weather, even in snow. I do remember one time when we were let out early because of a blizzard forecast.

— Chapter three —
COOKIE

Cookie was our dog when I lived on the farm, a spotted English Setter. Cookie was a great dog. He once got in trouble because he was chasing a deer. When my dad caught him in the act, he spanked him with a newspaper.

One time Cookie bit me in the face. I interrupted him when he was eating and got a bit too close to his face. He bit me and left tooth marks on my forehead.

We lost Cookie one fateful day when I was at school. Cookie was chasing a car when another dog, also chasing the car, pushed Cookie underneath the car tire. I saw it all happen. Cookie tried to climb out of the ditch where he had fallen after being run over, but he couldn't climb out and died right there. That was a very sad day for me.

— CHAPTER FOUR —
HARVEST TIME

Every year in late summer came harvest time. Whether it was wheat or oats, dad would get the combine ready to harvest the crop. Usually, my dad's uncle would also come with his combine to help. This was a special time of year when everybody available would help with the harvest. I helped by driving tractor pulling a grain trailer. When full, the grain trailers were pulled, by tractor, to the grain bins or shed. Dad purchased two metal grain bins used for either oats or wheat. We also had an old log cabin type shed which also held grain.

The grain trailers were pulled to the bins and shed, and then grain was transferred by a special grain augur to the bins and shed. I would sometimes jump around in the oats or wheat grain trailers. It felt good on my feet when I took my shoes off and jumped around in the grain, but I remember how the oats would make me itch.

Mice were a problem in the grain bins. Sometimes I would open the top of the grain bin and mice would scurry everywhere.

— Chapter Five —
RIDING TRACTORS

It was not unusual for an eight to ten-year-old, maybe even younger, to drive tractors around the farm. Even running hay rakes and hay balers was not uncommon. My brother John was two years older than me, and he got to run the hay baler when he was probably only 10 years old. I remember driving tractor while my dad and brothers loaded hay onto hay wagons. I also remember driving the tractor pulling grain trailers. One event in particular stands out. I was pulling a grain trailer with the tractor when I approached my dad's combine to get a load of grain. Unfortunately, I got a little too close to the combine and rubbed tires with it. The look on my dad's face told the story. He thought I was going to plow right into the combine itself, but I only grazed it.

— CHAPTER SIX —
WAR BATTLES
WITH ARMY SOLDIERS

My older brother and I spent a lot of time playing war games with small army soldiers. One year for Christmas (or my birthday?), which unfortunately is only five days after Christmas, I requested a set of revolutionary plastic war soldiers. The British soldiers were red, and the American soldiers were blue. My brother John and I would set up our soldiers amidst blocks of wood that we used for cover. Then we stretched rubber bands across combs or rulers and shot them at the opponent's soldiers. We spent hours playing war games, and we also played with green army soldiers and Indian figures.

We had a plastic fort with sentry boxes at each corner. We set up army men inside the fort and then placed Indian warriors outside to attack the fort, again using rubber bands on combs or one-foot rulers as weapons.

We spent hours battling one another with our toy soldiers and toy Indians. Sometimes we played outside, setting up lines of battle in the gravel on our driveway. We made trenches in the gravel and used weeds as if they were trees for our soldiers to hide behind.

We also had a toy barn with farm animals and plastic fencing. We played "farming" with toy animals, tractors, and plows. This was usually outside, so we could farm actual soil using toy tractors and plows. What a great childhood we had!

— Chapter Seven —
ICE ON THE RIVERS AND PONDS

One of the things I loved to do in the winter time was ice skate. The creeks and ponds froze over, and skating along in the middle of creeks and rivers was always fun. Being outside in nature was cool! We would skate Kettle River and sometimes travel long distances. I remember one time, I heard the ice crack underneath my feet. I quickly jumped to the bank as the ice broke in the creek.

Another time, my oldest brother Ron, who was eight years older than me, decided to build an ice pond in our backyard. He piled up snow in a rectangular shape and then ran water through a hose to fill up the pond with water that later froze into ice. Then we played ice hockey on our new ice pond. What fun!

Our time on the Minnesota farm was filled with outdoor activity. We did not have cell phones or any other type of electronics. Social media was unknown to us. We were the better for it.

— Chapter Eight —
SQUIRRELS IN THE TREES

One of the most entertaining things my brother John and I did as young Minnesota farm boys was use homemade slingshots to try to knock grey squirrels out of oak treetops. Usually, it was an exercise in futility. The squirrels were smart and would hide on the backside of limbs.

Our slingshots were made by finding a crotch of a limb, cutting it to fit the hand, then using rubber inner tube strips as the elastic "slings." The pouch for holding the rocks was made from leather.

Back to the squirrels. We spent long hours "slinging" for squirrels. Even if we were lucky enough to hit a squirrel, it usually wasn't enough to knock it out of the oak tree. I don't remember ever killing a grey squirrel although we tried our best to do so. I do remember wounding a red squirrel once. He was in a smaller tree, and I got lucky with my slingshot and hit him in the head with a rock. It knocked him out of the tree, but I think he survived.

— Chapter Nine —
The Deer

One early summer evening as my brother John and I walked home from crow hunting, we were amazed to see a dozen or more deer eating alfalfa behind our pole barn. Boy, were we excited! There were huge buck deer with antlers and several does as well. We hurried home, trying to stay crouched down so we would not scare the deer away. We ran into the house yelling, "Come look at the deer behind the pole barn!" So the whole family hurried out to the pole barn, and from there we could look out the windows and see the deer fairly close to us. They seemed unalarmed and content to just eat alfalfa hay.

Neighbors came over to watch the deer as word got out of their presence. This happened nearly every evening for several weeks, and sometimes up to 20 deer would be there. Of course, by hunting season, the deer were long gone!

— CHAPTER TEN —
CROW HUNTING

My brother John and I often hunted crows. Back in those days it was legal to shoot them; in fact, the state of Minnesota even had a bounty on crows. All you had to do to claim the bounty was cut off one leg of the crow and send it in for redemption. One crow's foot was worth 50 cents. That was big money to a kid back then. We only had a .22caliber semiautomatic rifle between the two of us, but it worked pretty well if we could find a crow sitting long enough to shoot at it. There were woods on our property in two different places, and crows were common back then. One time my dad lined up two crows in the field and with one shot, killed them both with his .218 B rifle. That was cool!

Another time when we were crow hunting, a large flock of crows went wild, squawking and flying all around us. We hovered under a large fir tree. It seemed like they knew we were trying to shoot them. They kept flying and squawking until we finally left the sanctuary of the fir tree and went home!

— CHAPTER ELEVEN —
SNOW IGLOOS

Minnesota always got its share of snow and ice. A favorite thing to do was cut snow blocks and make igloos in the snow. Then we would crawl inside the igloos and pretend we were Eskimos. Life was great growing up on a Minnesota turkey farm! Very little time was spent watching TV. Instead, kids used their imaginations. It was truly life in the 50s, and we were a Leave It to Beaver household.

— Chapter Twelve —
CHURCH ON SUNDAYS

Our family was a "Sunday go to church" family. We attended Bethany Lutheran Church. There were a lot of Lutherans in Minnesota. I remember Sunday school and especially the hymns. I had a good ear for music and a good voice. My maternal grandfather was buried in the church cemetery.

Besides church music, my dad played accordion and was in a small musician group made up of one or two guitar players (my uncles) and a violin or fiddle player who also played the saw. It was a regular wood saw that he made "sing" with the fiddle bow. This "band" was pretty good at making music, mostly waltzes and polkas along with Christmas tunes. I always sang along with the Christmas tunes!

— CHAPTER THIRTEEN —
WOOD BURNING KITCHEN STOVE

We had a wood burning kitchen stove on which Mom baked bread and cooked turkeys. I loved dropping wood ticks on the hot iron of the wood burning stove. There were a lot of ticks in Minnesota, and whenever I would find one on myself, I dropped it on the wood stove and watched it fry.

The washing machine was also in the kitchen. Mom didn't have a clothes dryer. In the summer months, she hung clothes outside on a clothesline; in the winter months, they hung on a clothesline in the kitchen. The washing machine was the old-fashioned ringer type with rollers to press the water out of the clothes. I used to help mom by feeding wet clothes through the washer rollers. I used to be afraid of getting my fingers or hands caught in the rollers. And, of course, there were horror stories of kids getting caught in the rollers up to their arm pits!

— Chapter Fourteen —
WILD DOGS

Dad hated untrained, undisciplined stray dogs that raised havoc with the turkeys. I remember one time when a couple of stray dogs came on our property. Dad grabbed his .218 B rifle and shot one as it approached the turkeys. A stream of blood poured from the dog's head as dad and I approached it. Of course the dog was dead before it even bled out.

— CHAPTER FIFTEEN —
DEER HUNTING

My dad was rather famous as a good shot with the rifle. He was especially good at hunting Minnesota white tail deer. A huge, many antlered Buck Whitetail hung in the garage on the wall. Story has it that it dressed out at over 200 pounds. That's a large deer! Whitetail hunting was popular in Minnesota. People came from out of state to hunt whitetails in Minnesota.

Normally, hunters drove wood lots, pushing deer out to the open fields where posted hunters would shoot them. My great uncle was lost during hunting and shot by another hunter. No one ever knew who the other hunter was because several hunters were shooting all at once when my uncle was hit by a stray bullet.

— Chapter Sixteen —
GRANDPA AND GRANDMA CRANDELL

My maternal grandparents lived a rather primitive lifestyle. No indoor plumbing or indoor toilets. Water was secured by operating the hand pump on the porch. Usually the pump needed to be primed so you had to have water on hand. The water was clean and cold and tasted great. There was an outdoor privy toward the barn. It was rough going out there especially in the winter time.

They had no electricity either, but rather used old-fashioned kerosene lanterns to give off the needed light in the evenings. Us kids would play cards and board games by the light of the lanterns after dark.

— CHAPTER SEVENTEEN —
DEAD TURKEYS

One of the most enduring memories of my farm life was the stench that came from dead turkeys. Dad had a concrete bin with a lid on it to hold them. It would never fill up because maggots devoured the dead turkeys' flesh first. When we opened the lid to drop in the dead turkeys, it smelled awful, and, of course, seeing the millions of maggots crawling all over the turkeys was a sight to behold. I had nightmares of somehow falling into the bin and being eaten up by maggots. Not a pleasant dream!

Turkeys died from diseases or from predators. Skunks and red foxes were a problem. Dad and my oldest brother Ron used to hunt for red foxes. They weren't protected back then but probably are now. Skunks, of course, were shot whenever we saw them. One time, dad shot a skunk in the driveway not far from the house. He said the skunk let loose a blast of spray as it died. It smelled terrible. Dad ran hose water over the spray to try to alleviate the smell, but it didn't work that well!

— Chapter Eighteen —
TURKEYS AREN'T
THAT SMART

Rumor has it, turkeys have been known to drown just from looking up during a rainstorm. I pretty much believe it. They are not the brightest of God's creatures. One amazing thing was when a flock of gobblers (male turkeys) were together, one gobble would set off the whole flock gobbling. It was instantaneous. The first gobble was barely out of the turkey's mouth when the whole flock would gobble.

Turkeys are also not bright when it comes to lying down for the night. Some turkeys would bed down next to the woven wire fence they were enclosed in. Unfortunately, skunks or foxes would come along and grab them and eat them on the spot!

— CHAPTER NINETEEN —
DAD'S INGENUITY

I already mentioned that my dad was a crack shot when it came to deer hunting. Another time his proficiency at shooting was helpful was when he decided to add a grain augur to the concrete silo. Instead of using some type of concrete cutting tool, dad used a 30:06 rifle to shoot out the hole through which the new augur would be placed. It worked amazingly well! Dad would set up the rifle on a bench about 50 yards away and continue shooting until a large enough hole was made for the augur. He placed the grain augur through the hole and then spread black tar around the augur to seal out the rain and moisture.

— Chapter Twenty —
TRACTOR RACES

One time when the folks weren't home, my brother John and I were challenged by my older brother Ron and his friend Jimmy Steirna to a race with the tractors. John and I had the old Moline tractor while Ron and Jimmy had the newer Moline tractor. The race track was the country roads that made up a square mile around ours and the neighbors' farm. It wasn't much of a race given the difference in the tractors, but John and I did give them a run for their money. We were still competitive on the backside of the square mile, but Ron and Jimmy gradually pulled away from us. What a thrill!

We entertained ourselves on the farm. We didn't need TV or social media to keep life interesting. WE made life interesting ourselves.

— CHAPTER TWENTY-ONE —
TADPOLES AND MUD DAUBER WASPS

Nature was my playground growing up in Minnesota. Whether it was tadpoles in mud puddles or wasps in the mud, everything in the natural world around me was interesting to behold.

Tadpoles grew concentrated together as spring mud puddles from the snow melt began to dry up. It was fun catching them and then watching as they matured into full-blown frogs. The mud wasps were targets to hit with rocks or other projectiles I managed to hurl at them. I probably shouldn't have tried to kill them, but they were enemies because of their stings.

— Chapter Twenty-Two —
RUNNING BEHIND
THE OLD TRUCK

The old water truck was a source of great fun! My brother John and I would grab onto the end boards of the truck bed and hang on as my dad or older brother Ron drove it to water turkeys in the field. The old truck didn't go fast, so we could keep up with it by hanging on and running behind it. If we got tired of running, we would lift our legs and feet up to a cross member and just hang on as the truck sped along.

Many parents today would not allow kids to do what we did, but it was great fun! The danger added to the excitement!

— Chapter Twenty-Three —
ANTS IN THE SAND

Nature was always at our fingertips on the farm. One of the things I did to entertain myself was watch ants going to and from their home in the gravelly and sandy ground. There were many small mounds where ants came to and from their underground nest. Ants are creatures of great strength. I watched them carry kernels of sand that surely outweighed them.

To get a better view, my brother John and I constructed ant farms. These were made by sliding two sheets of glass ¼ inch apart into wood frames with grooves for the glass. Then we added sand and ants to the frames. Thus, we could see the ants as they made tunnels and stored food underground. This was great entertainment. No need for TV and video games on the farm. We made our own entertainment!

— Chapter Twenty-Four —
BASEBALL

Where we lived Minnesota in the 50s there was no organized Little League baseball, but that didn't stop my brother John and me from playing. We played catch a lot and also practiced batting as we pitched to each other. We had only wooden bats back then. I sometimes used rocks to practice batting, throwing them up in the air and then hitting them as they came down. Occasionally, we even played baseball with my older brother Ron and his friends, even though they were much older than us.

Our favorite team to watch on TV or listen to on the radio was, of course, the Minnesota Twins. During my 10 years in Minnesota, there was only one time that I got to a Minnesota Twins game in person. They played at home, hosting the New York Yankees. The Yankees had Yogi Berra, Mickey Mantle, Roger Maris and other star players like Whitey Ford and Billy Martin. The Twins had Harmon Killebrew and Bobby Allison.

— Chapter Twenty-Five —
SPUTNIK

I well remember the thrill of seeing the Sputnik satellite orbiting the earth in the nighttime sky. Our whole family went outside in the Minnesota farmland darkness to see the satellite. Because there was little or no light pollution in the central Minnesota farm country, The Milky Way in all its glory stood out brightly. The Sputnik satellite also was easy to spot as there were no other satellites in the sky, and we were not in a jet airplane pathway. My family marveled at the history-making satellite; we were all excited about it. My siblings and I wanted to be the first to spot Sputnik. I don't remember who spotted it first, but I do remember seeing it clearly and watching it traverse the sky.

— Chapter Twenty-Six —
CUBAN MISSILE CRISIS

The look on my father's face told the story. I remember watching the black and white TV broadcast as President John F. Kennedy told the American people about the Cuban missiles and the American response to blockade Russian ships to Cuba. My dad's face was white with fear. I probably didn't understand the seriousness of the event, but I'll never forget my dad's face!

— Chapter Twenty-Seven —
MILITARY PLANE FLYOVERS

In the late 50s and early 60s military jets flew over our farm regularly. They were apparently testing radar, especially trying to fly below radar tracking capabilities. They would fly very low over our farm, and the sound was deafening. We could hear them coming and usually us kids would run outside to see them. B-52's, B-48's and B-58 fighter bombers all flew right over our house and farm. Sometimes they dropped shredded aluminum foil, which was probably a radar tracking diversion tactic.

I liked the B-58's the most. They were a fighter bomber type plane. It seemed to me anyway that they were louder than the other planes.

— Chapter Twenty-Eight —
GEESE HEADING SOUTH

Our 160-acre farm was right under the bird migration central flyway, a migration route that birds of all kinds followed. The geese were most visible. Sometime in late fall great flocks of geese flew over on their way south for the winter. I think I missed my calling. I should have become a naturalist for all the nature experiences I had as a young Minnesota farm boy.

My brother John and I are now in our 60s. We are both into bird watching or "birding" as it is called. The birding started when we were young farm boys. We bought a map-like birding chart with pictures of Midwest birds. The chart came with cards with pictures of individual birds. We could match the cards with the chart. The Bobolink was my favorite bird back then. I liked the sound of its name, and also, we had Bobolinks right there with us on the farm.

— Chapter Twenty-Nine —
BILLY SMITH

Billy Smith was a friend of our neighbors. He was a few years older than me. One day we were loading hay bales on the hay trailer, pulled by a tractor driven by my older brother, Ron. Somehow Billy Smith got himself caught between the tire of the trailer and its frame. Fortunately, Ron stopped quickly and prevented a real catastrophe.

Billy had tire marks across his belly where the tire of the trailer had rubbed him. The only other "injury" was that Billy crapped his pants. We all had a laugh over that, well, except Billy. I think he learned to stay away from tractor and trailer tires!

— Chapter Thirty —
HILLVIEW STORE

A few miles south of the farm was a grocery store called The Hillview Store. Harvey Stierna and his wife Martha ran the place. They were good friends with Mom and Dad. We often went to the store to visit the Stierna family. They lived in the back part of the store which was made up of a kitchen, living room, and bedrooms. Jimmy Stierna was their son, who was the same age as my brother Ron, and they had an older daughter named Bernice.

I remember playing hide and seek often on the outside of the store especially after dark. We also played cards or watched dad and Harvey play cards with the older boys, Ron and Jimmy.

— CHAPTER THIRTY-ONE —
NORTHERN LIGHTS

The family farm in Minnesota was north enough to see Aurora Borealis or the Northern Lights. They were most common in the fall or winter months. What a beautiful sight they were, beautiful colors that danced in the nighttime clear skies of Minnesota.

— Chapter Thirty-Two —
PISTOLS FOR CHRISTMAS

My brothers and I once found the stash of Christmas gifts hidden in the closet, so, of course, we snooped inside the boxes. This particular Christmas, we found toy pistols. These were special pistols, especially the one for Ron. His pistol had actual shells with brass casings and lead bullets. You cold load them up with paper powder rolls, so when you pulled the trigger, there was a loud bang and smoke that came out of the barrel.

My brother John and I got pistols also, but they weren't so special. They didn't have the life like bullets but did have the paper powder roll set up, so we could make lots of noise and smoke.

— Chapter Thirty-Three —
HALLOWEEN
TRICK-OR-TREATING

Living in the country made for limited trick-or-treating on Halloween. It was such a distance between houses that we had to walk quite a while to trick-or-treat!

One Halloween mom bought us special noisemakers, which we enthusiastically used as we walked from one country house to another. The weather was cool, and the skies were clear. The moon was full and bright, and the Milky Way was glorious! My siblings and I walked several miles that Halloween night. Two of the homes we visited were our cousins' families, so we spent a little extra time there warming up.

— Chapter Thirty-Four —
MIDWEST HUMIDITY

During the hot summer months, Minnesota nights were warm and humid. We had no air conditioning back then, so we had to endure the humidity without it. Opening the windows in my bedroom offered some relief, but not much. I can still remember sweating in my bed at night. It just didn't cool down. We just had to endure it and count the sweat drops.

— Chapter Thirty-Five —
MINNESOTA MOSQUITOES

It's been said that the Minnesota state bird should be the mosquito! I don't know if Midwest mosquitos are bigger than others, but it sure seemed like it. They were numerous for sure. They say Minnesota has 10,000 lakes, and many of them are mosquito breeding ponds and swamps.

— Chapter Thirty-Six —
DEBEAKING TURKEYS

My dad was quite an innovator. Or maybe I should say "inventor." Dad built a turkey debeaking machine from scratch. Turkeys are notorious for pecking any wound or flaw on their neighbor's body. Therefore, it was necessary to cut or partially remove the top beak of the young turkeys. The debeaking machine was simple in design. The young turkey was held facing the machine, its mouth pressed against a rod, separating its beak. The cutting part of the machine was electrified, so it removed and seared the top beak of the turkey, which was the part responsible for the pecking damage. This process did not harm the turkey at all, other than possibly a little bit of pain from the cutting.

Debeaking several thousand turkeys one at a time was a lengthy process. My siblings and I would round up the turkeys and herd them into a waiting pen from which my dad would grab them one at a time for debeaking. It was a long but necessary job.

— Chapter Thirty-Seven —
EGG RUNS

My dad had hen turkeys which laid fertile eggs. Every two weeks or so, Dad loaded up all the eggs and took them to Detroit Lakes to the turkey nursery plant. I loved going with him because the staff at the egg nursery plant gave me jelly filled donuts.

The plant had huge incubation chambers where the fertile eggs were placed. They rotated around until the eggs hatched. Then the chicks were loaded into containers to go back to the turkey farms.

— Chapter Thirty-Eight —
NINE LIVES

My brothers and sisters used to say that I was like a cat with nine lives. The first life was before I was born when my mother lifted a heavy anvil when she was pregnant with me. This caused problems with the pregnancy, and I was lucky to be born alive. My second life was when I was a toddler and followed my dad in his car as he attempted to pull into the garage. It was a sharp corner into the garage, and Dad backed up to realign his vehicle with the garage door opening. He heard a thump and opened his door to pull me up from under his car. I somehow missed being run over by his car tire. The third life was my previous story with the turkey water truck. My fourth life was when I was distracted by pulling a chain on the garage roof. It was a flat roof, and, for some reason, I was up there pulling this chain. I pulled the chain backwards and stepped right off the edge of the garage roof which was 10 feet high. I landed on my back and all I got was a cut lip from my teeth biting it. My fifth life was later out west when I crashed my bicycle into a barbed wire fence and got cuts on my right arm and right leg... 240 stitches worth of cuts. I bled like a stuck pig. So far, I have not had any other close calls, but for a while, we all wondered!

— Chapter Thirty-Nine —
COUSINS

One of the most fun times of life on the farm was when the cousins came over. I had a lot of cousins, but they didn't visit that often, so when they did, it was a real treat. One time when several of the cousins were at our house, my cousin Russ barely escaped a tragedy. It happened this way. Several of us were together at a garbage pit. One of my cousins found an old pitchfork minus the wood handle. For some reason he threw it, and it bounced off a rock right into my cousin Russ's face. One of the sharp points of the pitchfork poked Russ right between the eyes. His parents took him to emergency care, but it was just a superficial flesh wound. It didn't penetrate the skull, fortunately.

— Chapter Forty —
VISITING GRANDMA HASBARGEN

Before the family moved out west, we went to visit Grandma Hasbargen. She lived a ways away, so we didn't go see her very often. It was a little scary for a young guy because she was bedridden and missing several teeth. She had fallen and broken her hip and, from then on, was bedridden. Grandma Hasbargen knitted while in bed. She always knitted gloves for the grandchildren and great grandchildren, and we wore these gloves during the winter snow season. Grandma Hasbargen was a devout Christian, and she prayed for her family regularly. She lived to be 100 years old and spent a lot of time praying for all her children, grandchildren and great grandchildren. I credit her with the fact that I came to have faith in Christ. Her prayers brought a lot of people to faith in Christ.

— CHAPTER FORTY-ONE —
WHIRLPOOLS

Every spring the whirlpools appeared. Snow melt fed rushing waters along the ditches of the county road we lived on. And sure enough, at the culverts, where water flowed from one side of the road to the other, whirlpools formed. I used to have nightmares about falling into a whirlpool and being sucked underneath the waters and transported into the culverts and lost forever. Such is the imagination of a young Minnesota farm boy.

— CHAPTER FORTY-TWO —
TWO OF NINE LIVES LOST

Out west, there were two incidents that were close calls. The first was when we had just moved. I was still only 10 years old. My brother and a cousin and I had built small boats, and we were bicycling to a small creek nearby to try them out. The creek was at the bottom of a hill about ½ mile from our house. My brother and cousin rode on ahead of me. I was pedaling along when suddenly my boat came loose from the luggage rack. As I turned to look back at the boat, I steered my bicycle to the right and scraped along the barbed wire fence near the road. Needless to say, I got pretty well cut up on my right arm and leg. I had over 240 stitches worth of cuts, some quite deep.

When I saw the cuts on my arm, I yelled to my brother and cousin. Then I went running to the closest house, the home of John Potter, one of my dad's coworkers at Linton Plywood Mill in Oregon. Jean Potter, John's wife, was in her bathrobe at the kitchen table sipping on her coffee, when I came running to the door. Their dog bit me in the rear as I ran to the house, but even that didn't slow me down! Jean grabbed some bath towels and wrapped my arm. It wasn't until my brother got there that I even realized my leg was cut, when he pointed it out to me and Mrs. Potter.

Mr. Potter loaded me up in his truck and drove me home. Mom and dad quickly took me to the hospital, and the doctors put me under to do the stitching.

Mrs. Potter told us later that she didn't panic at all until after I left, and she had trouble holding her coffee cup still. She also had a mess of blood all over her kitchen floor.

The second incident was when I was older, 19 or 20, when my good friend Chuck Rydie and I decided to climb Mt. Hood for the second time. Our first ascent was the southern route, going straight up the mountain from Timberline Lodge. We made it up and down in six hours. For our second ascent, we decided we would try a slightly harder route on the west side of the mountain. We didn't have a map but just headed up and over to the west side of the mountain. Somewhere about half way up, we realized we were in trouble. The path got steeper and steeper, and we soon found that we wouldn't be able to go down the way we came up. Chuck prayed and asked God to help us. We had crampons, ice axes, and rope but no pitons or other climbing gear. Chuck led the way. A great peace settled over us. I call it a presence or angelic helper.

As the climb got steeper, occasionally a rock would work loose from Chuck's climbing. He would yell "rock" and I would move out of the way as it passed me by. It was surreal! God's angels were helping us. Finally, we got to the last part of the climb, and it was vertical. We prayed again for God's help, and Chuck again led the way up. He made it to the top and had to literally pull me up the steep slope. We made it to the top of the west side. The summit was across the way on the other side of the mountain. We didn't even bother to summit that day; we felt confident we had accomplished our goal of conquering the western route.

— CHAPTER FORTY-THREE —
HERE KITTY KITTY KITTY...

My mother used to tell of the time when my oldest brother Ron found a new kitty cat to play with. My oldest brother was eight years older than me. He was just a toddler when mother heard him say, "Here kitty, kitty, kitty." She went outside to investigate, and sure enough, Ron was following a kitten saying, "Here kitty, kitty, kitty, only this was not a regular kitten; this was a skunk kitten! Fortunately, nobody got sprayed.

— Chapter Forty-Four —
Cousin Allan

My cousin Alan Matta had a rough time at our farm in Minnesota. One year when his family was visiting, he was riding a bike and fell over and broke his arm.

Another time when he was visiting, we were walking down a dirt road, and Alan was pushing a bat-sized stick in front of him. More specifically he was pushing the stick with his groin. All went well until the end of the stick got stuck on some vegetation in the dirt road. Of course, it jammed him in the groin and was very painful!

Another time when my cousins came over, we four boys went to an abandoned farmhouse and barn where we found old newspapers, really old ones from WWII. We brought them home and showed them to our parents, who weren't too thrilled that we were going inside abandoned farmhouses and barns.

— CHAPTER FORTY-FIVE —
BUTCHERING TURKEYS

Being raised on a turkey farm meant we had plenty of turkeys to eat, whatever the season. I used to help my mother butcher the turkeys. We would do it in the kitchen where we used a large bin to soak the turkeys. Soaking the turkeys in hot water made it easier to pull the feathers out.

Once the feathers were pulled out, we sliced open the turkeys to remove the entrails. What a terrible smell that was. Sometimes we found fully developed eggs inside the hen turkeys. That was amazing to me.

In case you are wondering, the butchering actually began by chopping the live turkeys' heads off with an axe or hatchet over a block of wood. I was always amazed at how long the headless turkeys would flop around, sometimes for a minute or more.

— Chapter Forty-Six —
The Old Barn

The old barn on the farm was always an interesting place to hang out. Before I was born, dad used to milk cows in the old barn. Then he got into the turkey business. Dad built two new pole barns to house the turkeys. Eventually, a private contractor tore the barn down and took the wood for his pay.

— CHAPTER FORTY-SEVEN —
CATCHING BIRDS

There were always lots of birds around the farm, especially English (House) Sparrows and Juncos or "Snowbirds" as they were called. I used to try to catch these birds. I used a cardboard box and a stick with a long string attached to it. I would place birdseed on the ground and wait until birds came to eat it. Then I held the box up with the stick and when a bird hopped under the box, I would pull the string. It never worked too well because the birds were quick and usually flew away out of reach of the box.

My cousin Curtis Hasbargen had a homemade sparrow trap that worked a lot better than the box and stick method I had tried. It was designed to catch birds alive and several at a time. It was comprised of a weight-activated elevator that would lower under the weight of a single bird. The bird then crawled through a one-way hatch into a holding pen. Once one bird was caught, other birds were attracted to the trap, so several birds could be trapped at once. This trap mainly designed to catch English Sparrows, which were abundant around turkey farms. They were considered a pest bird and were not protected under federal law as were other songbirds.

— Chapter Forty-Eight —
Old Fashioned Telephones

We had an old telephone on a party line, which meant we could listen in on other people's conversations. We called it rubbernecking.

The telephone was the old wooden box style with an earpiece and a mouth piece into which we would listen and/or talk. I believe our phone number was "one short" and "two long" rings.

One time during hunting season, my grandma Johnson called to let dad know there were deer feeding in a hay field on her property. My dad and brother Ron grabbed their guns and went to shoot the deer. Unfortunately, they found my cousins had beat them there, and they had already shot the deer. How did they know about the deer? They listened in on the conversation or "rubbernecked" when my grandmother called my dad.

Closing Thoughts...

In the dictionary, musings are defined as meditations, reflections, or contemplations. I have included in my writings reflections on the life I lived as a child. My hope is that you, the reader, will get a glimpse into my life and see, especially you baby boomers, the beauty of Midwest farm life in the 50s and 60s. It was life before the internet, smart phones, tablets, and video games. I wouldn't trade my life on the farm for any of the modern entertainment gadgets that my children and grandchildren use. Bring back simplicity, quietness, and family in contrast to the hectic, accelerated lifestyle of today. My hope is that Musings of a Minnesota Farm Boy will begin in you that attempt to get back to the joys and blessings of the simpler life. Enjoy the journey!

Manufactured by Amazon.ca
Acheson, AB

15901871R00035